Creative
HANDPAINTED
BEARS

by Annette Stevenson

Creative
HOUSE

CONTENTS

CONTENTS

This book is dedicated to my Dad, John McNally, who always encouraged and supported me in everything that I chose to do with my life.

Published by Creative House
(an imprint of Sally Milner Publishing Pty Ltd)
PO Box 2104
Bowral NSW 2576
AUSTRALIA

©Annette Stevenson

National Library of Australia Cataloguing-in-Publication data:
Stevenson, Annette.
   Creative handpainted bears.

   ISBN 1 877080 02 0.

   1. Teddy bears. 2. Decorative arts. 3. Painting - Technique. I. Title.

758.96887243

EDITORIAL
Managing Editor: Judy Poulos
Editorial Assistant: Ella Martin
Editorial Coordinator: Margaret Kelly
Photography: Neil Lorimer
Styling: Judy Ostergard
Illustrations: Lesley Griffith

DESIGN AND PRODUCTION
Production Manager: Anna Maguire
Design: Jenny Nossal
Cover Design: Jenny Pace
Production Editor: Sheridan Packer
Design Manager: Drew Buckmaster

Printed in China
Reprinted 1998, 1999, 1999, 2000, 2002

INTRODUCTION

Teddy bears occupy a special place in our hearts and in our memories. An essential part of our childhood years, teddy bears have stayed with many of us as much-loved companions into adulthood.

Annette Stevenson has loved and collected bears for most of her life. Now, as an accomplished decorative artist, she sees it as a challenge to bring them to life with a few strokes of her paintbrush.

Over the years, I have developed many different ways of painting my bears. From the fuzzy, woolly bear to the long-haired, shaggy bear to the old, worn, much-loved relic, they are all rendered with loving attention to detail, and each one with a unique personality of its own. In fact, the bears in my collection have inspired many of the designs in the book.

Each design is shown in full colour and with a step-by-step workboard to follow, enabling even beginners to paint a special bear of their own.

This delightful book is for all lovers of teddy bears.

Annette

ABOUT THE AUTHOR

Annette Stevenson has always had an interest in art, graduating with a Diploma of Arts after leaving school. About eight years ago, she became interested in decorative painting, bought some paint and brushes and has never looked back. For the last six years, she has been a popular and sought-after teacher, bringing her delightful painted bears to an ever-widening audience.

PREPARATION AND FINISHING

STAINING

My preferred wooden surface for painting is pine and I usually stain it, because I love the beautiful grain of the wood. To make the light stain, mix Jo Sonja's Artists Acrylic Gouache, Brown Earth, Jo Sonja's Retarder and Antiquing Medium and Jo Sonja's All-Purpose Sealer in equal parts. Mix this up in an old jar with a lid – it keeps for ages if sealed properly. The depth of colour can be varied by adding more or less Brown Earth acrylic paint. Brush this mix on with a large base-coating brush and wipe it immediately with a soft, clean cloth.

For the darker stain used in many of the projects, mix equal parts of Dark Walnut and Cherry Liquitex Wood Stain. Apply this over the light stain, using a sponge brush and brushing in the direction of the grain. This looks great if you allow the stain to remain streaky. Do not wipe this stain with a cloth.

BASE PAINTING

I use a good quality 1" base-coating brush and sand lightly between coats. Matisse Background Paint in Pale Beige is my favourite base-painting colour, and I give my pieces four coats to obtain a nice even finish.

ANTIQUING

Antiquing a piece will give it a gentle aged effect that would normally take years to achieve. It is also useful for subduing some of the bright colours used.

Firstly, apply a coat of patina to your piece using a soft cloth, then rub Burnt Umber oil paint all over the entire surface to be antiqued. Gently wipe this off with a soft cloth, softening the edges. A large mop brush is also useful for softening edges.

VARNISHING

I use Cabots Crystal Clear Varnish in a satin finish. Apply three or four coats with a good quality flat brush, sanding very lightly between coats. It's a good idea to keep one brush just for varnishing. If your piece has been antiqued, use J.W.'s Right Step Satin Varnish as Cabots Varnish will not adhere over the oil paint.

BRUSH TECHNIQUES

I generally float shading and high lighting using a size 12 flat brush. Dip the brush into the water basin and gently blot it on a paper towel to remove the excess water. Load the paint onto one corner of the brush and blend well on your palette. When shading or highlighting with floated colour, always use your brush flat and with the colour next to the area you want shaded or highlighted. If you want to mix two colours together to highlight, load both colours onto the same corner of the brush and blend them back and forth on the palette to mix them. This will give you a variation in colour every time, which adds interest to the final piece.

TRANSFERRING THE DESIGN

The painting designs for each project are given with the instructions or, in the case of the very large pieces, on the Pull Out Pattern Sheet. Many of the designs have been reduced for space reasons. Simply enlarge them on a photocopier to the full size.

To transfer the design, first enlarge it, then trace it onto suitably coloured graphite paper. Centre the design on the piece to be painted and, using a stylus, draw over the design, transferring the outline onto the wood.

MATERIALS

PAINTS

I like to use a variety of brands of paints for my projects as they each have different colours and qualities. The brands used in this book are Jo Sonja's Artists Acrylic Gouache for the bears; Matisse Professional Artists Acrylic Colour (mainly Burgundy as it is a wonderful rich colour and matches well with my dark stain) and DecoArt Americana, because they have a great range of soft pinks, apricots and cream for roses and clothes.

PALETTE

I use waxed disposable palette paper. This is available at art supply stores in pads of fifty pages. The paint does dry out more quickly than if a wet palette is used, but dry paint is better for painting these bears. If you want to preserve the paints for later use, cover them with plastic kitchen wrap.

BRUSHES

I used a variety of brushes for the projects in this book. I usually buy Loew-Cornell brushes as they perform very well and last a long time. Take good care of your brushes – you can't expect to do a wonderful painting using a tired old brush. For the furry bears, I use Neef 440 deerfoot brushes in a variety of sizes. For the long-haired bears, I use Loew-Cornell rake brushes, series 7120.

PAPER TOWEL

A good quality paper towel is used to blot or wipe brushes on. Kitchen wipes, such as Chux, are also handy for wiping brushes.

OTHER ITEMS

Other supplies that are useful in your painting kit are:
- stylus (for tracing patterns and making dots)
- white chalk (for sketching in roses or clothes)
- graphite paper, white and blue
- kneadable eraser
- sharpener
- pencil
- cotton buds
- soft cloth (for antiquing or staining)
- fine sandpaper, 320 grade
- coarse sandpaper, 120 grade
- tack cloth

LONG-HAIRED BEAR

This bear differs from the fuzzy bear in that the fur is created using two rake brushes and lots of little lines to make it look soft and cuddly.

Jo Sonja's Clear Glazing Medium helps to blend the paint and gives you longer to work with it. Load the brush in the medium before loading it in the paint. The brush is loaded only on the very tip of the bristles and used in a criss-cross manner to create the effect of soft lines. The first brush is used for the two shade colours and the second brush for the two highlight colours. This bear is worked in sections, so that you have time to play with the paint.

These bears take a little more practice to achieve a pleasing look than the fuzzy bears, so I would advise you to paint a couple of practice ones first on a sample board. Painting on a board feels totally different to painting on paper.

The way I change the colours of these bears is to wait until my work is completely dry, then mix a small amount of paint with Jo Sonja's Clear Glazing Medium and apply a wash over the whole bear. Yellow Oxide for a light bear and Burnt Sienna for a dark one. You could try some colour combinations of your own to see what effect you can achieve. Have fun and persevere.

PALETTE

Jo Sonja's Artists Acrylic Gouache:
  Raw Sienna, Gold Oxide, Yellow
  Oxide, Brown Earth, Warm White,
  Burnt Umber
Jo Sonja's Clear Glazing Medium

PAINTING

STEP ONE

Using a size 10 filbert brush, casually base paint in the bear in sections (arms, head, tummy) with Raw Sienna and a small amount of Clear Glazing Medium.

STEP TWO

Load the dirty brush in Brown Earth and apply the shading. This is placed where the body parts of the bear meet. If the arm is in front of the tummy, the shading would be placed onto the tummy, right next to the arm. The workboard will show you where to put the shadows.

STEP THREE

Using the two rake brushes, apply the fur in the manner described above. The first brush is loaded in Clear Glazing Medium, then Gold Oxide. Apply the shading in a crosshatched manner, working the colour well into the base colour. There should not be a definite line where the two colours meet.

STEP FOUR

Wipe the brush on a paper towel and proceed to load in the shade colour, Brown Earth. Add extra depth in the places that would be darkest, using only a small amount of this colour and blending it well into the Gold Oxide shading. Remember to always use Clear Glazing Medium before each colour to help blend the paint. You can work for quite a while on each step before the paint starts to dry.

STEP FIVE

Using the second brush loaded in Yellow Oxide, start to build up the highlights. The highlights are worked from the outside of the bear towards the inside, using the brush in a flicking motion so you produce lots of fine, little lines.

STEP SIX

Wipe the brush on a paper towel to remove the excess paint and pick up a small amount of Warm White. Add these highlights to the very outside edges of the bear.

STEP SEVEN

Base paint the pads of the feet in a mix of Raw Sienna, Brown Earth and Warm White, using a size 10 filbert brush. Side-load the same brush in Brown Earth and shade the pads in a couple of places, usually near the bottom of the foot.

STEP EIGHT

Paint the eyes and the nose with a small round brush and Burnt Umber. Paint lots of connecting small lines so that you end up with an uneven shape to look like some of the hair is falling across the eyes and nose.

Annette Stevenson ©96

Annette Stevenson © 96

FUZZY BEAR

This bear is a really furry little fellow and my favourite bear to paint. He can be painted in many different colours but I like him best in the old-fashioned mustard colour.

Variations for the colours of this basic bear are: for a light bear, base paint in Yellow Oxide, shade with Burnt Sienna and highlight with Warm White and a small amount of Yellow Oxide. For a darker bear, base paint in Burnt Sienna, shade with a mix of Brown Earth and Burnt Umber and highlight with a mix of Yellow Oxide, Burnt Sienna and Warm White.

I hope that you enjoy this old favourite of mine.

PALETTE

Jo Sonja's Artists Acrylic Gouache: Raw Sienna, Burnt Sienna, Brown Earth, Yellow Oxide, Warm White, Burnt Umber

PAINTING

STEP ONE

Load a size 10 filbert brush in Raw Sienna and base coat the bear in sections – for example, the ears, arms and head. By doing it this way, it is easy to see the pattern lines through the paint, ready for the next step. This does not need to be a solid coat of paint – the patchy effect achieved with one coat of paint will add to the look of the finished bear.

STEP TWO

Side-load the same brush in Brown Earth, blend well on the palette and pat in the shading. These shadows do not need to be neat – short choppy strokes will be fine. Follow the step-by-step workboard for a guide to where the shadows are placed.

STEP THREE

Now the fun part – adding the fur. Using the three deerfoot brushes, stipple or pounce lightly over the base-coloured bear, using Raw Sienna with the first brush. Do not make it too heavy.
Note: I use three deerfoot brushes: the first brush is for the base colour, the second for the two shade colours and the third for the two highlight colours. I use three brushes so that I don't have to wet the brushes, because I don't use any water in this style of bear painting. The brush is always used dry and the fur is applied with a pouncing or stippling motion, using the full flat of the brush. It is very important that the brushes are not washed, until the bear is totally finished.

STEP FOUR

Reinforce the shadows with the second brush, loaded in Burnt Sienna. Using Brown Earth, add extra depth onto the parts of the bear that are darkest – under the chin, around the pads of the feet and where the arms join the tummy. These are all painted using the second brush.

STEP FIVE

Finally, add highlights in the same manner. Using Yellow Oxide and a small amount of Warm White mixed on the palette, very lightly pounce along the edges of the bear. It is important to see three values of colour at this stage of painting. With the same brush, add a few extra Warm White highlights to the outside edges, paying particular attention to the muzzle and the tops of the ears. Do not add too much white, to retain the mustard colour. Try not to blend the fur too much – this is a fuzzy bear not a smooth, blended bear. This way of painting fur should also be painted one area at a time, in the same way as the base painting, so that the colours remain wet and there is the chance to work with the paint before it dries.

STEP SIX

Paint the eyes and nose using Burnt Umber and a small round or flat brush. Pat in the eyes and nose rather than painting them with conventional strokes. This way they will be an uneven shape and give the effect of the fur coming over them.

Annette Stevenson © 96

OLD ORIGINAL BEAR

This old bear is a firm favourite of mine as he reminds me of my old bear, Big Ted, that I was given when I was born. He was first given to my brother John, then passed on to my sister Pauline, and then it was my turn to love him. However, by the time I received him he had no fur (John ate it), one eye was missing and he had a couple of patches!

This type of old bear is painted with no fur but you can create different fabric effects by placing prewashed calico or kitchen wipes over the wet paint to make a pattern. This looks like holes where the fur has been pulled out.

PALETTE

Jo Sonja's Artists Acrylic Gouache:
   Yellow Oxide, Brown Earth, Warm White, Burnt Sienna, Burnt Umber, Gold Oxide
Jo Sonja's Clear Glazing Medium

PAINTING

STEP ONE

Begin by loading a size 10 filbert brush in Yellow Oxide and base paint in the bear's shape. This does not need to be a solid coat of paint.

STEP TWO

Side-load a size 8 flat brush in Gold Oxide and float in the shading. Try to have this shading smooth and even. Place a few extra patches here and there to look like rips in the fabric and patches. Repeat this step using Brown Earth to create dark shadows. The main areas for dark shadows are under the chin and on the feet, depending on how the little fellow is sitting.

STEP THREE

Side-load a size 8 flat brush in a 1:1 mix of Warm White and Yellow Oxide and add some highlights to the edges of the bear on the tops of the ears, top of the head, tops of the feet, middle of the tummy and on one side of the arms. Big Ted already looks quite good at this stage and he could be left like this with some liner work to roughen up the edges.

STEP FOUR

Mix a small amount of Burnt Sienna with the glazing medium and, working on one area at a time, base paint over the previous work, making sure that the areas are dry. Work very quickly so that the maximum effect can be obtained from this step. Lay the kitchen wipes or calico over the wet area and rub gently, lift off and see the small pattern that remains. If you are not happy with this, base paint again with the glazing mix and try again. Try a few different fabrics to see what patterns you can make. Allow this to dry really well.

STEP FIVE

Side-load a large flat brush, one that you are comfortable working with, in Burnt Umber and redefine the shadows, making sure that there are a few lumps and bumps here and there to give him a pre-loved look. I don't do any more than this, but you could experiment with some liner work in Burnt Umber, if you want to try something different.

STEP SIX

Add some lines in Burnt Umber for his eyes and nose, a few stitching lines around any shaded patches and your own Big Ted is completed.

Annette
Stevenson
©96

ROSES

The inspiration for these roses came from Julie Neilson-Kelly. I was so inspired by her roses that I developed a way of painting them in a more simplified form. They are to be a suggestion of a rose, rather than a very complex one.

PALETTE

DecoArt Americana Acrylic Paint, Buttermilk

Jo Sonja's Artists Acrylic Gouache: Warm White, Paynes Gray, Teal Green

FolkArt Acrylic Colors: Cinnamon, Peach Perfection

STEP ONE

Double-load a size 12 flat brush in Buttermilk and Peach Perfection. Blend this well on your palette until there is a third value in between. Base paint the bowl of the rose with the cream towards the top. Feather in the top petals and block in the side and bottom petals with the light colour to the outside.

STEP TWO

Side-load your dirty brush in Cinnamon and add depth to the throat of the rose and around one side of the bowl. Repeat, using some Paynes Gray at the bottom of the bowl.

STEP THREE

Do not wash your brush. Load it in some Teal Green and block in the leaves. Put your brush down flat, twist onto the chisel edge and lift off.

STEP FOUR

Highlight the rose with a dry-brush method, using Buttermilk. The paint should be dry so the petals appear to be wispy and light. If water is added to the paint, the strokes will disappear. Try to make these strokes very light. Keep them running in the direction of the petals, starting from the outside.

STEP FIVE

Repeat Step Four using Warm White, but not as much – just a few strokes here and there.

STEP SIX

Mix some Peach Perfection and Teal Green and use it to add some negative foliage or filler leaves. These are comma strokes made with the flat brush and lots of water to fill in any gaps.

Annette
Stevenson
© 96

THE BOYS

This chest was painted for my only son, Samuel, with all the characters that a boy loves.

MATERIALS

Large pine toy chest, 38 cm x 66 cm x 35 cm (15 in x 26 in x 13½ in)
Liquitex Wood Stain: Dark walnut, Cherry
Three deerfoot brushes, size ⅜
Two rake brushes, size ⅜
Flat brushes, sizes 4, 10 and 12
1" base-coating brush
Fine liner brush
Jo Sonja's Clear Glazing Medium
Jo Sonja's Retarder and Antiquing Medium
Jo Sonja's All Purpose Sealer
Jo Sonja's Artists Acrylic Gouache: Raw Sienna, Yellow Oxide, Brown Earth, Burnt Sienna, Warm White, Burnt Umber, Paynes Gray, Carbon Black
DecoArt Americana Acrylic Paint: Country Red, Uniform Blue
Matisse Professional Artists Acrylic Colour, Burgundy
White transfer paper
Stylus
Tracing paper
Scotch Brite scourer
Soft cloth
Cabots Crystal Clear Varnish

PREPARATION

See the painting design on the Pull Out Pattern Sheet.

STEP ONE

Mix the light stain as instructed on page 5 and add a small amount of Raw Sienna. This makes the chest look more like Baltic pine. Make sure that you mix a large enough quantity of this stain as it will never be exactly the same colour when mixed again. Apply the stain with a nice wide brush or a large foam brush. Make sure you follow the grain and wipe off in the same direction. Work one area at a time as this stain will dry quickly. When it is dry, sand lightly with the Scotch Brite scourer to smooth the surface.

STEP TWO

Trace the design and transfer it centred onto the chest.

PAINTING

Note: All shading and highlighting is painted using the size 10 or 12 flat brush while floating the colour.

T-SHIRT BEAR

STEP ONE

This fellow is painted following the instructions for the Fuzzy Bear on page 10. Base paint in Burnt Sienna, shaded with a brush mix of Brown Earth and Burnt Umber. Highlights are a mix of Yellow Oxide, Burnt Sienna and Warm White. Add extra Warm White highlights with the same dirty brush.

STEP TWO

Base paint the T-shirt in alternating stripes of Paynes Gray and Warm White. This is easiest to do with the size 12 flat brush, working straight across the shirt. Float some shading using Paynes Gray down the edges of the body and sleeves using the same brush.

STEP THREE

Using a size 4 flat brush, add a smaller stripe of Warm White in the top stripe under his chin. Using the liner brush and Burgundy, write 'bear' in the centre. You could write your child's name instead.

Try to achieve a soft fur look when applying the highlights

17

STEP FOUR

Paint the eyes and nose using Burnt Umber and a highlight of Warm White.

OVERALL BEAR

STEP ONE

He is painted in the same colours as the basic Fuzzy Bear on page 10.

STEP TWO

Paint his overalls in a 1:1 mix of Uniform Blue and Paynes Gray. Shade with Paynes Gray to define the position of the pocket and straps. Pick up a small amount of Uniform Blue and Warm White and mix them on the palette. Use this mix for highlights. Add Warm White stitching lines around the straps and pocket, down the front imaginary seam and at the cuff of the pants. Add Country Red buttons to the bottom of the straps.

STEP THREE

Paint the eyes and nose using Burnt Umber and a highlight of Warm White.

SAILOR BEAR

STEP ONE

This bear is painted following the Long-haired Bear instructions on page 7.

STEP TWO

Base paint his hat and collar with two coats of Warm White. Add the stripes on the collar insert in alternating stripes of Warm White and Paynes Gray. Float the shading on the lower edge of the hat band and to separate the panels of the hat, using Paynes Gray. Paint shadows on the inside of the collar.

STEP THREE

Base paint the tie at the front of his collar and the button on the hat using Country Red, shaded with Burgundy. Paint a fine line in Country Red around the edge of the collar about 3 mm

(¹/₈ in) in from the edge. Paint Paynes Gray stitching lines on each seam of the hat.

STEP FOUR

Paint the eyes and nose using Burnt Umber and a highlight of Warm White.

FRONT OF CHEST

Base paint the lettering in a 1:1 mix of Uniform Blue and Paynes Gray. Float shadows down the left side of each letter with Paynes Gray. Float highlights down the right side of each letter using Uniform Blue and Warm White mixed together so it is a little lighter than the base colour.

BEARS

Both bears are painted in the same way as Fuzzy Bear on page 10, using the same colours.

TRAIN DRIVER BEAR

His hat and scarf are base painted with two coats of Warm White. Add shading in Paynes Gray to separate the band from the hat, and under his chin and around the knot of the scarf. Add the checks on the scarf randomly with Paynes Gray and a small flat brush. The lines on the top of the hat are also in this colour, following the curve of the hat and brim.

PIRATE BEAR

Base paint his hat and eyepatch with Carbon Black. Highlight around the top edges with a mix of Warm White and Carbon Black – this does not need to be too light. Base paint the crossbones with this light mix and add Warm White highlights, here and there.

FINISHING

STEP ONE

Using the 1" brush, base paint the routered edge on the lid of the chest and the board at the bottom with two coats of Paynes Gray.

STEP TWO

Apply at least four coats of varnish to cope with the rough-and-tumble of little boys playing.

The Train Driver Bear

The Pirate Bear

18

Annette Stevenson © 96

Annette
Stevenson
© 96

MADELEINE

The real Madeleine sits on the chest of drawers in my bedroom and was a very special present from my children. I have painted her on a lovely oval picture. She looks vulnerable and forlorn as though she has been left at the altar.

MATERIALS

Wooden oval picture frame, 42 cm x 52 cm (16½ in x 20½ in)
Flat brushes, sizes 4, 10 and 12
Two rake brushes, size ½
Deerfoot brush, size ¼
Liner brush
Jo Sonja's Clear Glazing Medium
Liquitex Wood Stain: Dark Walnut, Cherry
Matisse Background Paint, Pale Beige
Treasure Gold, Classic
Jo Sonja's Artists Acrylic Gouache: Raw Sienna, Brown Earth, Gold Oxide, Yellow Oxide, Burnt Sienna, Warm White, Pine Green, Burnt Umber
DecoArt Americana Acrylic Paint: Shade Flesh, Buttermilk, Crimson Tide
Matisse Professional Artists Acrylic Colour, Burgundy
Antiquing patina
Oil paint, Burnt Umber
White transfer paper
Pencil
Stylus
Sandpaper, 320 grade
Tracing paper, A4 size
Water-based varnish, satin finish

PREPARATION

See the painting design on page 26.

STEP ONE

Mix the two Liquitex stain colours together in about equal proportions and stain the inside oval section (see page 5 for general instructions for staining).

STEP TWO

Base paint the outside edges of the frame with four coats of Pale Beige. Sand well between coats, paying particular attention to any routered edges of the frame. When these coats are dry, base paint the outside edge and the back of the frame with two coats of Burgundy. Also, base paint the small routered edge of the oval in Burgundy.

STEP THREE

Trace the design and transfer it onto the oval board. Note that the bow sits off the edge in the top right-hand area of the oval.

PAINTING

CHEST OF DRAWERS

STEP ONE

With the large flat brush, streak some watery Brown Earth over the entire drawers. Side-load in the Burnt Umber and float this colour on the drawers and the sections in between them.

STEP TWO

Side-load in Raw Sienna and float highlights of this colour on the top edges of the drawers. Streak some of this colour across the front of the drawers.

STEP THREE

Using the size 4 flat brush, shade and highlight the knobs with the same two colours as before. Add final highlights to the drawers and knobs, using a mix of Raw Sienna and Warm White.

MADELEINE

STEP ONE

Paint her following the instructions for a Long-haired Bear on page 7. Do not paint the eyes at this time. Dry well and apply a coat of the Glazing Medium.

STEP TWO

With the rake brush loaded in the glazing medium and a small amount of Warm White, add extra fur. These strokes need to be really soft and light, running in all directions. This step can be repeated as many times as you want until you are happy with the result – usually three or four times is sufficient to give a nice, soft appearance. Allow the paint to dry completely.

STEP THREE

Load the size 12 flat brush in glazing medium and a small amount of Burnt Sienna and add some extra shadows where necessary. Do not do too much as this will make Madeleine look too dark. If she does begin to look dark, you can reverse the process and glaze with Warm White.

STEP FOUR

Base paint Madeleine's eyes and nose with Burnt Umber, then add highlights with Buttermilk. Float some Burnt Umber around the edge of the eyes, making it look patchy, not even and smooth. The best way to paint this is to have your flat brush at right angles to the eye and keep lifting the brush up and down so that the float is wiggly along the edge of the eye.

BOW

The bow is floated in following the design, using Buttermilk. The strongest colour should be on the pattern lines. Add Warm White to create the soft folds of the bow.

BOUQUET OF ROSES

The roses are painted in the same way as on the workboard for roses on page 16, but using the following colours: the base is Buttermilk and Shade Flesh, shaded with Crimson Tide and Pine Green, used separately. The highlights are Buttermilk first, then Warm White. The leaves and buds are added using Pine Green and a touch of Shade Flesh.

GYPSOPHILA

STEP ONE

Add the vine around the neck and through the bouquet using watery Burnt Umber and the liner brush. I use a short liner as I find I have more control over my strokes with it.

STEP TWO

Paint the leaves with Pine Green, using the size 4 flat brush.

STEP THREE

Dab in the flowers, using the size $1/4$ deerfoot brush and Buttermilk. Repeat this here and there, using Warm White.

FINISHING

STEP ONE

Antique the Pale Beige part of the frame, using the patina and Burnt Umber oil paint. This should not be too dark – just enough to soften the overall look of the finished picture.

STEP TWO

Rub a little Treasure Gold around the routered edges.

STEP THREE

Finish with four coats of varnish.

Light strokes running in all directions create the soft fur on this bear

MADELEINE
Painting Design
Note that the design is given at half size.
Enlarge it on a photocopier at 200%.

JACK, THE HURT TEDDY

The poor little fellow has been in the wars; he needs some special care and a great big hug. I gave this little bear to my dad a few years ago when he had a hip operation. Jack is one of my favourites and holds many special memories.

MATERIALS

Pine medicine cupboard, 40 cm x
   35 cm x 14 cm x 40 cm
   (15½ in x 14 in x 16 in)
Check stencil
Three deerfoot brushes, size ³/₈
Plastic kitchen wrap
Flat brushes, sizes 2, 8 and 12
Round brush, size 2
Fine liner brush
Stencil brush, any size
1" base-coating brush
1" sponge brush
Matisse Background Paint,
   Pale Beige
Liquitex Wood Stain: Dark Walnut,
   Cherry
Jo Sonja's Artists Acrylic Gouache:
   Raw Sienna, Burnt Sienna, Brown
   Earth, Yellow Oxide, Warm White,
   Burnt Umber, Smoked Pearl,
   Carbon Black
Magic Tape
Water-based varnish
Sandpaper, 320 grade
Blue graphite paper
Stylus
Tracing paper, A4 size

PREPARATION

See the painting design on page 28.

STEP ONE

Stain the cupboard with a mix of Dark Walnut and Cherry. I have made this slightly lighter than my other stained pieces by putting more Cherry in the stain mix.

STEP TWO

Using the 1" base-coating brush, base paint the inner panel of the door with three coats of Pale Beige, sanding lightly between coats.

STEP THREE

Attach the stencil in place using the Magic Tape. Using the stencil brush and Raw Sienna, stencil in the checks. Not much paint is required to do this as it looks best if the cream background colour shows through the painted checks.

STEP FOUR

Trace the bear pattern and transfer it onto the middle of the door.

PAINTING

STEP ONE

Paint Jack, following the instructions for Fuzzy Bear on page 10. I have used two shading colours for this fellow: Burnt Sienna, then Brown Earth in places to deepen the shadows. Try to use a small amount of paint and gradually build up the shadows and highlights as this will make a much softer-looking bear.

STEP TWO

Paint the bandage around his head, using the size 8 flat brush and Smoked Pearl. Give this area a nice even coat.

Smudge the edges of the bandage to soften them

STEP THREE

Scrunch up a small piece of plastic kitchen wrap, making sure that you finish with a point on the top. Dab this into Warm White, then dab it over the bandage. It doesn't matter if this looks fuzzy around the edges as it gives the bandage a more realistic look. When this is dry, gently float some Brown Earth along the lower edge, using the size 8 flat brush, to create the overlap of the bandage. At this stage, leave the safety pin out as it is better to paint both pins at the same time.

STEP FOUR

Paint the sling with two coats of Smoked Pearl. Allow to dry. Float Brown Earth shading and gathers at the neck and elbow, using the size 12 flat brush. For the gathers, slide the chisel edge of the brush to create jagged lines. Using the same brush, float Warm White highlights along the outside edges. I have also cross-hatched a touch of highlight into the centre parts of the sling.

STEP FIVE

Base paint the bandage around his foot with Smoked Pearl. Shade and highlight, using the same colours as for the sling. Make sure your shading is in curved lines around the foot, instead of straight across, making it look like the bandage is wrapped around his foot.

STEP SIX

Base paint the crutch in a mix of Raw Sienna and a touch of Warm White. Float Brown Earth shading along the lower edges and around the top of the crutch. Float a highlight of Warm White along the top edges and pat a touch of highlight into the centre of the top of the crutch. The rubber knob on the bottom is based with watery Burnt Sienna and shaded with Brown Earth.

STEP SEVEN

Base paint the safety pins with a mix of Warm White and Carbon Black – a middle-value grey. Using the size 2 flat brush side-loaded in Carbon Black, float a touch of shadow here and there. If this is too dark, you may like to add a highlight with Warm White, as well.

FINISHING

Varnish the cupboard. When it's dry, put all your bandages inside it to take care of life's little mishaps.

JACK, THE HURT TEDDY
Painting Design
Note that the design is given at half size. Enlarge it on a photocopier at 200%.

Annette Stevenson
© 97

FRIENDSHIP PLAQUE

This dome-shaped plaque has a collection of my favourite teddy friends and toys all together. The finished piece has been antiqued to give the impression of a past era.

MATERIALS

Large wooden plaque
Three deerfoot brushes, size $^3/_8$
Three deerfoot brushes, size $^1/_4$
Two rake brushes, size $^3/_8$
Deerfoot brush, size $^1/_8$
Round brush, size 3 or 4
Fine liner brush
Flat brushes, sizes 2, 4 and 12
Antiquing patina and cloth
Oil paint, Burnt Umber
Jo Sonja's Artists Acrylic Gouache: Raw
    Sienna, Brown Earth, Yellow Oxide,
    Burnt Sienna, Warm White, Fawn,
    Smoked Pearl, Gold Oxide, Paynes
    Gray, Teal Green, Jade, Burnt Umber,
    Carbon Black, Rose Pink, Opal
DecoArt Americana Acrylic Paint,
    Buttermilk
Matisse Professional Artists Acrylic
    Colour, Burgundy
Matisse Background Paint,
    Pale Beige
Jo Sonja's Clear Glazing Medium
Treasure Gold, Classic
Blue graphite paper and stylus
Tracing paper, A3 size
J.W.'s Right Step Varnish, satin finish

PREPARATION

See the painting design on the Pull Out Pattern Sheet.

STEP ONE

Base paint the centre section of the plaque with three coats of Pale Beige, sanding lightly in between coats. Base paint the outer edge of the frame with two coats of Paynes Gray, sanding well on the routered edge.

STEP TWO

Trace the design and transfer it onto the plaque, using the graphite paper.

PAINTING

Hint: With this design, it is easiest to paint the bears or toys that are behind, first. I started with the long-haired bear with the checked bow in the middle of the group.

STEP ONE

Bear with the bow: Paint this bear following the Long-haired Bear instructions on page 7, using the same colours. When he is dry, glaze him with Yellow Oxide and glazing medium.

STEP TWO

T-shirt Bear: Base paint in Burnt Sienna, then shade with a mix of Burnt Umber and Brown Earth. Highlight with Yellow Oxide, Burnt Sienna and Warm White, with a touch of each mixed on the brush.

STEP THREE

Bear with the sailing boat: Base paint in Yellow Oxide, then shade in Burnt Sienna. Highlight with Warm White and a touch of Yellow Oxide.

STEP FOUR

Baby bear: Paint this bear in the same way as the bear with the T-shirt. Use the tiny deerfoot brush for this fellow.

The highlights help to make this bear's ear sit forward

Try to give each bear a different facial expression

STEP FIVE

Bear next to the ball: Paint this bear in the same colours as my basic bear: Raw Sienna and Brown Earth, with Warm White and Yellow Oxide for the highlights. Use the size ¹/₄ deerfoot brush for him.

STEP SIX

Bear next to the block: Base paint with a mix of Fawn and Smoked Pearl and shade with a 1:1 mix of Fawn and Brown Earth. Highlight with Smoked Pearl first, then Warm White.

STEP SEVEN

Mammie doll: Base paint her face and hands with Burnt Umber. Her dress is Buttermilk, shaded with a float of Raw Sienna. Pick up some Warm White on the edge of your brush and pat in some highlights to the centre of each section of her dress. The lines on her skirt and sleeves are watery Burgundy. Add a stitching line around the edge of the yoke of her dress using the same colour. Paint the rags on her head, randomly around, using Burgundy and Paynes Gray. Add Buttermilk checks to the blue rags, and add dots to the Burgundy ones. Her hair is wispy lines of Burnt Umber and the heart on her dress is Paynes Gray.

STEP EIGHT

Rag doll: Base paint her face, hand and feet with Opal, shade lightly with Fawn and add a touch of highlight to the top edges, using Warm White. Paint a fine Burnt Umber stitching line around the face, hand and feet. Base paint her dress and bow with Fawn, shaded with Brown Earth and highlighted with a mix of Fawn and Smoked Pearl. The collar and apron are Buttermilk, shaded with Raw Sienna and with a Warm White highlight around the edge. Base paint her hat with Carbon Black, base this right next to her head as the hair is painted over this area later. The collar and apron have a thick check of Paynes Gray. I used the size 2 flat brush for this check. The fine line between the checks is Burgundy

and the stitching line and cross are Paynes Gray. Paint her hair using the ¹/₄ deerfoot brush, using Burnt Sienna first, then Raw Sienna.

STEP NINE

Beach ball: Base paint with Raw Sienna and Burgundy. Shade the Raw Sienna stripes with Brown Earth and the Burgundy stripes with Burnt Umber. Add a touch of highlight here and there with Yellow Oxide and Buttermilk. The stars are Burnt Umber and the fine lines are Jade Green.

STEP TEN

T-shirt: Base paint with alternating stripes of Buttermilk and Teal Green. Shade with Teal Green and paint the lettering with Burgundy.

STEP ELEVEN

Oval box: Base paint with Smoked Pearl with Teal Green for the grass. Shade around the lid and along the sides in Paynes Gray, taking this roughly halfway down the sides, as it will be the sky. Float the lower section with Teal Green for the grass. Pat Warm White on the top and sides of the lid for highlights. The trunks of the trees are Brown Earth. Stipple the foliage with Teal Green, then Jade. Paint the lettering in Paynes Gray and the hearts in Burgundy.

STEP TWELVE

Checked bow: Base paint the bow in Burgundy. Highlight in Burgundy and Buttermilk. Add Buttermilk checks.

STEP THIRTEEN

Baby bear: Paint her bib using Buttermilk. Float a ruffle around the edge and add a Burgundy heart.

STEP FOURTEEN

Sailboat: Paint the hull and mast with Raw Sienna. Shade with Brown Earth and highlight the top edges with Raw Sienna and Warm White. Base paint the sails with Warm White. Float Paynes Gray closest to the mast and along the

lower edge. Add extra Warm White to the outside edges.

STEP FIFTEEN

Paint a small bow on the bear on the right-hand end in Teal Green and Buttermilk, mixed together. Add a touch of Buttermilk for highlights.

STEP SIXTEEN

Alphabet block: Base paint with Raw Sienna and shade with Brown Earth. Float Yellow Oxide and Warm White on the edges for a little highlight. Paint the lettering in Burgundy, using the size 2 flat brush. Paint the fine lines around all the edges in Paynes Gray.

STEP SEVENTEEN

Quilt: Base paint the large squares in Buttermilk and the large stripes in Paynes Gray. Float some Raw Sienna around the edges of the squares. Highlight all the stripes with a mix of Paynes Gray and Buttermilk. Paint the hearts in Burgundy and the leaves in Teal Green. The button is Buttermilk with a couple of small dots in Burnt Umber. Add a Paynes Gray stitching line around all edges of the squares.

STEP EIGHTEEN

Paint the verse on the plaque with watery Burnt Umber.

FINISHING

STEP ONE

Antique the whole plaque with Burnt Umber oil paint, following the instructions for antiquing on page 5. I then rubbed the plaque to wipe off the colour in the highlighted areas on the dolls and bears, and softened all the outside edges.

STEP TWO

Rub Treasure Gold carefully around the routered edge of the frame with a soft clean cloth, then varnish with several coats.

Friendship

Annette
Stevenson
©96

Annette Stevenson © 96

FRANCOISE

This budding artist is painted on my brush box and he's just right to take to my classes. The box is craftwood and has no grain, but you can create the grain by streaking some extra stain onto the sides after the entire piece has had its first coat of stain.

MATERIALS

Brush box 22 cm x 27 cm x 6 cm
  (8½ in x 11 in x 2½ in)
Flat brushes, sizes 10 and 12
Round brush, size 4
Liner brush, size 0
Script liner brush, size 1
Three deerfoot brushes, size ³/₈
Jo Sonja's Artists Acrylic Gouache:
  Raw Sienna, Burnt Umber, Brown
  Earth, Yellow Oxide, Warm White,
  Carbon Black, Pine Green, Sapphire, Teal Green
Matisse Professional Artists Acrylic
  Colours, Burgundy
DecoArt Americana Acrylic Paint,
  Sand
Check stencil
Stencil brush
Magic Tape
Matisse Background Paint, Pale Beige
Blue graphite or transfer paper
Stylus
Tracing paper, A4 size
Cabot's Crystal Clear Varnish,
  satin finish

PREPARATION

See the painting design on page 40.

STEP ONE

Using the dark stain mix, stain all the box inside and out. When this is dry, add extra streaks to the sides and soften them slightly.

STEP TWO

Mask the top of the box using the Magic Tape. I have left a 2.5 cm (1 in) border around this box, but the size would depend on the size of your brush box. Base paint this area with three coats of Pale Beige.

STEP THREE

Remove the tape and position the check stencil. Dab in the checks lightly so that the background colour still shows through.

STEP FOUR

Trace the design, then transfer it onto the lid of the box, using the graphite paper and stylus. Note that his feet overlap into the stained area.

PAINTING

THE BEAR

Paint the bear referring to the instructions and colours of Fuzzy Bear on page 10. Remember to use a small amount of paint, making sure that the shadows are placed on the correct parts of the bear.

BERET

Base paint with Carbon Black and float in a highlight around the two top edges using grey, made from two parts Warm White to one part Carbon Black.

SMOCK

Paint with two coats of Pine Green. Float shading using Pine Green and a touch of Black, side-loaded on the largest flat brush. Paint the lace around the edge of the smock and the dots using Carbon Black.

BOW

Paint with Burgundy, then shade with Burgundy and Black, brush-mixed together. Highlight with the base colour and Sand mixed together with a touch of each at the corner of the brush. Paint the checks with Sand, painting the vertical ones first, then the horizontal ones. Watery paint helps with fine liner work.

PALETTE

Paint in Raw Sienna and shade with a float of Brown Earth. Highlight with Yellow Oxide first, then a touch of Warm White. The puddles of paint are added, using the round brush and Warm White, Burgundy, Pine Green, Yellow Oxide and Sapphire.

PAINTBRUSH

Base paint with Carbon Black, using the round brush. While the paint is still wet, pick up some Warm White and blend it on the palette. Use this for highlights. Pat these two colours well to blend them. Paint the bristles with the liner brush, using the brown colours from your palette.

FINISHING

STEP ONE

Using the script liner and watery paint, paint a Burgundy line around the edge of the cream inset on the lid and a Pine Green line 1 cm (¹/₂ in) inside it.

Hint: You could use a tool for painting fine lines, such as the DecoArt Fine Liner Paint Writer which is a little bottle with a nozzle on the end. Mix the paint to an ink-like consistency and fill the bottle. Replace the lid and paint the lines, using the bevelled edge of a ruler to guide you.

STEP TWO

Varnish your paint box, then load your brushes into their new home, ready to take to class.

Watery paint helps to create fine liner work

FRANCOISE
Painting Design
Note that the painting design is given at half size. Enlarge it on a photocopier at 200%.

Annette Stevenson
© 96

CLAIRE

Claire is my very own grumpy bear. She is possibly the hardest to paint as the colours are patted in all over to gradually build up the shadows and highlights. She is sitting on a chair, dressed in her Sunday best, but I'm sure she would much rather be outside playing! The book box that she is painted on has been heavily distressed to make it look old and much used.

MATERIALS

Large wooden book box, 28 cm x 23 cm x 5 cm (11 in x 9 in x 2 in)
Flat brushes, sizes 2, 4, 10, 12
Round brush, size 3
Liner brush, size 1
1" flat brush
1" sponge brush
Selection of old fluffy brushes – I use old filberts
Jo Sonja's Artists Acrylic Gouache: Raw Sienna, Brown Earth, Yellow Oxide, Burnt Sienna, Burnt Umber, Warm White, Jade Green, Teal Green, Rich Gold
DecoArt Americana Acrylic Paint: Mauve, Buttermilk
Matisse Professional Artists Acrylic Colours, Burgundy
Matisse Background Paint, Pale Beige
Jo Sonja's Decor Crackle Medium
Sandpaper, 320 grade
Paper towel
Blue graphite or transfer paper
Stylus
Tracing paper, A4 size
Cabot's Crystal Clear Varnish, satin finish

PREPARATION

See the painting design on page 45.

STEP ONE

Base paint the outside of the box with three or four coats of Pale Beige, sanding lightly between coats. Using a 2:1 mix of Teal Green and Jade Green, base paint the inside of the box. Save some of this mix for finishing around the edges.

STEP TWO

Brush the crackle medium randomly along the spine of the book and also along the 'pages'. This will take about twenty minutes to dry – it should feel just tacky when touched with your finger.

STEP THREE

Very carefully apply the green mix to these areas – not too thickly as it is nice to see cream showing through where there are no cracks. Using the 1" base-coating brush with the green mix loaded just on the tip, stroke the paint from the edge into the centre and along the sides of the front cover. Make this really streaky. Allow it to dry well.

STEP FOUR

Sand the edges heavily and really distress the front cover to make it appear well-worn and old. Finally, rub some Rich Gold along the spine, 'pages' and around the front and back edges.

STEP FIVE

Trace Claire and her little friend and transfer them onto the front cover. Do not transfer the bows yet.

PAINTING

STEP ONE

Base paint both bears with Raw Sienna, using an old worn brush in a size that you are comfortable with. I find a size 10 just right for Claire and a size 4 for her little friend. Base paint the chair, using the size 4 flat brush, with Brown Earth. Base paint Claire's dress with Burgundy, using the size 10 flat brush.

STEP TWO

Using the size 12 flat brush side-loaded in Burnt Umber, place some shadows on the chair, the dress and the bears. On Claire, the main shadows at this stage are inside the ears and to create the lines on the feet. The sleeves and bodice of the dress also need to be defined clearly, as do the edges of the chair.

STEP THREE

Reapply Raw Sienna, working one area at a time, picking up a small amount of Brown Earth on the side of the brush and patting in the shadows to separate the neck and arms, muzzle, pads of the feet and paws. Wipe your brush on a paper towel, then pick up a small amount of Yellow Oxide and pat this on to start building up the highlights. At this stage, the bears look very patchy

and you should be able to see the three definite colours used so far. At this stage it is also good to add a few Buttermilk highlights to Claire's dress, around the edges of the bodice, outside and bottom of her sleeves, lower edge of the dress and a few streaky lines to start forming the folds on her dress.

STEP FOUR

Transfer the bows. Base paint Claire's bow in Burgundy and her friend's in Mauve. Lightly tap some Raw Sienna back onto Claire, just to moisten the surface slightly. Reapply a touch of Yellow Oxide and pick up a small amount of Warm White. Dry-brush these highlights onto the edges of the ears, the top of the head and the muzzle. Pat some highlights into the centre of the legs, feet and paws. Work the baby bear in the same manner until you are pleased with the effect.

Note: This is the hardest style of bear to paint and she takes quite a bit of practice to achieve the right results. Once you have painted this style of bear a couple of times, you will be happy with your results.

STEP FIVE

Using the size 4 flat brush, float some Buttermilk highlights onto the outside edges of the chair and also on the bows. Add a few definite folds on her dress and sleeves. Float in the collar and add scallops using the liner brush and Buttermilk.

STEP SIX

Paint the roses with the size 2 flat brush, double-loaded in Mauve on one side and Buttermilk on the other. Blend well on the palette and dab in the rose.

Remember, these are just tiny flowers. Add leaves in a mix of Teal Green and Buttermilk, using the liner brush.

STEP SEVEN

Base paint the eyes in Brown Earth and shade the lower edge with Burnt Umber. Paint a fine Warm White line right around the eye. With the size 2 flat brush, float Burnt Umber around the outside of the eye on the top and left sides. Add Warm White highlights. Paint the nose in the same way.

Hint: To make Claire look grumpy, dry-brush some Warm White above her eyes and float a little Brown Earth underneath them.

FINISHING

Varnish with several coats of Cabot's Crystal Clear Varnish.

Gradually build up the highlights using small amounts of paint

CLAIRE
Painting Design
Note that the painting design is given at half size.
Enlarge it on a photocopier at 200%.

Very soft, white highlights give the eyes a sad appearance

CHEST OF DRAWERS

This piece is truly wonderful with lots of drawers and lots of bears everywhere. My favourite 'wood man' and friend made this superb piece for me. The bears on the drawers are all small furry bears, which are a little harder to paint than the larger ones, but great fun and really cute to dress. Experiment with the colours and clothes and create your own family of bears on a chest to keep all your treasures in. Obviously, you may not have a chest exactly like this one. Simply adapt the painting to suit your own piece of furniture.

I have painted this piece using lots of cream, burgundy and green tones as they match the room that this chest of drawers is sitting in. It would look just as nice in any other colours.

MATERIALS

Chest of drawers
Jo Sonja's Retarder and Antiquing
  Medium
Jo Sonja's All Purpose Sealer
Liquitex Wood Stain: Dark Walnut,
  Cherry
Three deerfoot brushes, size ¼
Flat brushes, sizes 4, 6, 8, 10
Fine, short liner brush
Round brush, size 3
1" sponge brush
Jo Sonja's Artists Acrylic Gouache:
  Raw Sienna, Brown Earth, Yellow
  Oxide, Warm White, Burnt Sienna,
  Burnt Umber, Teal Green, Paynes
  Gray, Fawn, Smoked Pearl
Matisse Professional Artists Acrylic
  Colour, Burgundy
DecoArt Americana Acrylic Paint:
  Sand, Mauve
White transfer or graphite paper
Stylus
Tracing paper, A4 size
Sandpaper, 320 grade
Water-based varnish

PREPARATION

See all the painting designs on pages 55-57.

STEP ONE

Mix a large quantity of light stain and stain the entire chest of drawers. Let this dry well, preferably overnight. Sand well.

STEP TWO

Stain the outside of the chest with an equal mix of the two Liquitex stains. Once again, allow this to dry really well before proceeding.

STEP THREE

Mix Paynes Gray and Teal Green in equal proportions and paint one coat of this colour on the front edges of the chest – the piece of wood that the drawers slide into. Keep some of this colour for the clothes on some of the bears. Sand back really well along all the edges – even back to the raw wood in a few places.

STEP FOUR

Remove the knobs from the drawers and set them aside until later. Trace the patterns, then transfer the bears onto the middle of each drawer as indicated in the photograph.

PAINTING

Note: All the bears on this piece are painted following the instructions for Fuzzy Bear on page 10, but they all use slightly different colour mixes. The instructions work from left to right on each drawer. All the eyes and noses are painted with Burnt Umber and a dry-brushed highlight of Warm White.

DRAWER ONE (TOP RIGHT)

Bear 1: Base paint in Raw Sienna and shade with Brown Earth. Highlight with Yellow Oxide and Warm White. Float in the collar with Sand, using the small flat brush. Add crosshatching with the same colour, using the liner brush. Add the dots with the stylus. Paint the bow using a 1:1:1 mix of Teal Green, Paynes Gray and Sand. I tipped my liner brush with Sand so that there is a small amount of highlight on the bow.

Bear 2: Base paint in Fawn and shade with Burnt Sienna. Highlight with a mix of Fawn and Smoked Pearl. Base paint the jumper and the bow with two coats of Burgundy. Float in highlights with a brush mix of Burgundy and Sand to separate the arms from the tummy. Paint the fine lines across the sleeves and on the bottom of the jumper with Sand. Paint the flower dots with the mix used for the bow on Bear 1 and the centres in Sand.

Little dot flowers finish Bear 2's jumper

DRAWER TWO (CENTRE LEFT)

Bear 3: Base paint in Burnt Sienna and shade with a mix of Burnt Umber and Brown Earth. Highlight with Burnt Sienna, Yellow Oxide and Warm White. Base paint his jumper with the same blue/green mix as used for the trim on the chest, then float in highlights with Sand. Paint the main pattern lines of the Fair Isle pattern in Sand, then paint the first diamond using Burgundy and the inner diamond in the blue/green mix and Sand mixed together. It's probably a good idea to pre-mix this colour, as it is used frequently through the design. Add small lines of Sand around the collar and cuffs for a band on his jumper.

Bear 4: Base paint in Yellow Oxide and shade with Burnt Sienna. Highlight with Warm White and a touch of Yellow Oxide. Paint her pinafore in Burgundy, then float in some highlights in Sand and Burgundy brush-mixed together. Add small hearts in Sand to the lower edge of her pinafore. I use a

really small flat brush for these. Base paint the collar and ribbon with two coats of Sand. Float some shading under her chin, inside the bow and along the edge of the ribbon with a double side-load of Raw Sienna and Burnt Umber. To finish her ribbon and bow, add fine Burgundy lines to make checks. The bow at her neck is painted using the blue/green mix.

DRAWER THREE (CENTRE RIGHT)

Bear 5: Base paint with a mix of Raw Sienna and Fawn, and shade with a mix of Fawn and Brown Earth. Highlight with Fawn and Smoked Pearl. Paint her dress and bow with a 2:1 mix of Teal Green and Sand. Float in a little shading with Teal Green to separate the arms from the body and float highlights, using Sand. To finish her dress and bow, add very fine lines in Sand, using the liner brush, to make checks. These have a small Burgundy cross where the checks meet.

Bear 6: Base paint in Yellow Oxide and shade in Burnt Sienna. Highlight in Warm White and a small amount of Yellow Oxide, brush-mixed. Paint her dress with two or three coats of Sand. Float in the shading with Raw Sienna and Burnt Umber, mixed together. The shading needs to be quite definite under her chin, to separate the frill from the dress and around her arms to make them appear in front of her dress. Add a touch of Warm White to the lower edge of the frill and to the bottom of her dress. Using the short liner brush, add scallops along the edge of the frill and the lower edge of her dress with Warm White. The dots are also Warm White. With the round brush, add the insertion ribbon using Burgundy. Paint her hat with Burgundy, highlighted with a brush mix of Sand and Burgundy. Paint the roses with the smallest flat brush, using Mauve, Sand and Burgundy with leaves in Teal Green and Sand. There is one rose on her hat and she is holding a posy of two roses.

Bear 7: Base paint in Raw Sienna and shade with Brown Earth. Highlight with Yellow Oxide and Warm White brush-mixed together. Paint his vest in Teal Green, highlighted with a float of Sand to separate the front sections and add to the peaks on the bottom. Randomly add little line flowers with Sand and a Burgundy dot in the centre. Base paint the collar with two coats of Sand, shaded with a mix of Burnt Umber and Raw Sienna. Add a highlight of Warm White along the edge. Paint his bow tie and the stitching line around his collar in Burgundy. Add a little highlight to the edge of the bow tie just to separate the bow.

DRAWER FOUR (BOTTOM LEFT)

Bear 8: Base paint in Raw Sienna and shade with Brown Earth. Highlight with a mix of Yellow Oxide and Warm White. Base paint his vest with Teal Green and highlight very lightly with Sand. Add the pockets with a float of Sand. The stitching line around the edge and the writing on the pockets are also Sand. The collar is Sand with a float of the previously used shading colours. Add a Burgundy bow tie and a stitching line on the collar.

Bear 9: Base paint in Burnt Sienna and shade with brush-mixed Brown Earth and Burnt Umber. Highlight with a mix of Yellow Oxide, Burnt Sienna and Warm White. Float in her collar and the ribbon using watery Sand, then add crosshatching lines and dots around the edge in the same colour. Paint a small rose in her hand.

Bear 10: Base paint in Fawn and shade with Burnt Sienna. Highlight with Smoked Pearl. Paint her pinafore using Teal Green and a touch of Paynes Gray and Sand. Float the shading using Teal Green. The highlights are Sand. Add a tartan check to her pinafore first with Sand lines down and across, then Burgundy ones in between. Paint the buttons in Sand with two little Burgundy dots in the middle. The collar is Sand. Add shading under her chin in Burnt Umber and Raw Sienna. The stitching line and bow are Burgundy.

Bear 11: Base painting, shading and highlighting are the same as for Bear 8 on this drawer. Float in her collar with Sand and add small scallops along the edge and to create a pattern on the collar. Add crosshatching lines inside some of these areas. Small dots are added to the point of the scallops to finish the collar. Base paint her hat with Burgundy, highlighted with Sand. Add two small roses on her hat.

WRITING

Paint the writing, using the size 6 flat brush, as you would with a calligraphy brush, sliding onto the chisel edge as you paint. This creates the fat and thin lines. Shade the letters with Teal Green and highlight with Sand. I have added a fine line of Sand to the drawers.

FINISHING

Varnish, using your favourite water-based varnish. I suggest four coats with a light sand in between.

Fill up the drawers with your favourite teddy treasures.

Lots of liner work and dots add interest to these bears

51

1

2

Annette ©'97

CHEST OF DRAWERS
Painting Design for Drawer 1
Note the painting design is given at half size.
Enlarge it on a photocopier at 200%.

CHEST OF DRAWERS
Painting Design for Drawer 2
Note the painting design is given at half size.
Enlarge it on a photocopier at 200%.

CHEST OF DRAWERS
Painting Design for Drawer 3
Note the painting design is given at half size.
Enlarge it on a photocopier at 200%.

CHEST OF DRAWERS
Painting Design for Drawer 4
Note the painting design is given at half size.
Enlarge it on a photocopier at 200%.

CHEST OF DRAWERS
Painting Design for the writing
Note the painting design is given at half size.
Enlarge it on a photocopier at 200%.

BLANKET CHEST

The preparation of this new blanket chest to give it an aged appearance takes a little time, but the finished result with these fat, cuddly bears is worth every bit of it.

MATERIALS

Large pine chest, approximately
38 cm x 66 cm x 35 cm
(15 in x 26½ in x 13½ in)
Flat brushes, sizes 8 or 10, and 12
Filbert brush, size 4
Dagger brush, size ³/₈
Fine liner brush
Three deerfoot brushes, size ³/₈
1" sponge brush
Sandpaper, 320 grade
Jo Sonja's Retarder and Antiquing
Medium
Jo Sonja's All Purpose Sealer
Liquitex Wood Satin: Dark Walnut,
Cherry
Jo Sonja's Artists Acrylic Gouache: Raw
Sienna, Burnt Sienna, Burnt Umber,
Brown Earth, Yellow Oxide, Warm
White, Teal Green, Paynes Gray
DecoArt Americana Acrylic Paint,
Buttermilk
Matisse Professional Artists Acrylic
Colour, Burgundy
FolkArt Acrylic Colors: Cinnamon,
Peach Perfection
Water-based varnish
White transfer paper
Tracing paper, A3 size
Stylus

PREPARATION

See the painting design on the Pull Out Pattern Sheet.

STEP ONE

Stain the whole chest with a mix of the light stain. Allow to dry.

STEP TWO

Varnish randomly. Allow to dry. Sand heavily to remove most of the varnish.

STEP THREE

Stain the chest using the dark stain mix of Walnut and Cherry. The purpose of adding the varnish between the two coats of stain is that the second coat of stain will not adhere as well where the varnish is still present and this gives the chest an aged appearance.

STEP FOUR

Trace the design and transfer it to the chest, but at this stage, do not trace the roses or the lace collars.

PAINTING

Note: Paint all the bears, following the instructions for Fuzzy Bear on page 10 – only the colours vary. Working from left to right across the lid of the blanket chest, paint the four bears in the colours given below.

STEP ONE

Bear 1: Base paint the bear in Raw Sienna and shade with Brown Earth. Highlight with a mix of Yellow Oxide and Warm White.

Bear 2: Base paint the bear in Yellow Oxide and shade with Burnt Sienna. Highlight with Warm White and a touch of Yellow Oxide.

Bear 3: Base paint with Burnt Sienna and shade with a mix of Brown Earth and Burnt Umber. Highlight with Yellow Oxide, Burnt Sienna and warm White mixed together.

Bear 4: This fellow is painted in the same way as Bear 1.

Many pouncing strokes with the deerfoot brush make this bear look cuddly

STEP TWO

Paint all the eyes and noses with Burnt Umber, highlighted with Warm White. **Hint:** When using mixes of paint, mix them with your brush and not into a puddle as this will achieve a slight variation in the finished bear.

STEP THREE

Transfer the bows and collars onto the bears, using the white transfer paper and the stylus.

STEP FOUR

Bear 2: Base paint the bow with two coats of Burgundy, using the size 10 flat brush. Float shading with Burnt Umber inside the loop of the bow, under the knot and down one side of the ribbon. Float in the highlights with Burgundy and Buttermilk, mixed on the brush. Add this to the top edges of the loop and down one side of the ribbon. Add the dot of Buttermilk randomly, using the filbert brush.

Bear 4: Paint his tie with two coats of Paynes Gray. Float in the shading with Burnt Umber. Highlight with a brush mix of Paynes Gray and Buttermilk. Paint the fine lines using the same mix as the highlight. Don't add any lines inside the bow loop – they make it hard to distinguish the inside of the loop.

Bears 1 and 3: Using the dagger brush and Buttermilk, float in the collars and bows. Float along the outside edges of the collars and bows. Add some more of this colour under the bears' chins. Using the size 12 flat brush, float in C stroke scallops along the lower edge of each collar, the top edges of the bows and along the lower edges of the bows. Paint thin crosshatching lines in the same colour, using watery paint and the liner brush. These lines are straight, not curved as with usual crosshatching. The little dots finish off the lace collars and bows. I do these with the large end of a stylus.

Hint: If you have never used a dagger brush, have a little practice before painting on your piece. This brush is a much easier way to float colour in a large area.

FRONT OF CHEST

Note: The bears are painted in the same way as Bear 1 and their collars are also the same.

SCROLL

Base paint with three smooth coats of Buttermilk. Float Burnt Umber along all edges of the scroll, using the dagger brush. Pull some of the paint out towards the centre while it is still wet.

ROSES

Paint the roses on the chest in the same way as in the general instructions for roses on page 15 and using the same colours. Bear 1 also has a rose in the middle of her bow, Bear 3 has one on her shoulder and the front of the chest has one at the top right and bottom left of the scroll.

VERSE

The verse on the scroll is painted using watery Burnt Umber and the liner brush. It is best to do this writing in your own style as it will look more natural.

FINISHING

STEP ONE

Paint the trim on the top routered edge and the lower border of the chest with two coats of Paynes Gray and Teal Green mixed together in equal proportions.

STEP TWO

Apply four coats of varnish. Place this lovely chest at the end of your bed for all to see.

Keep the roses and filler foliage soft and light

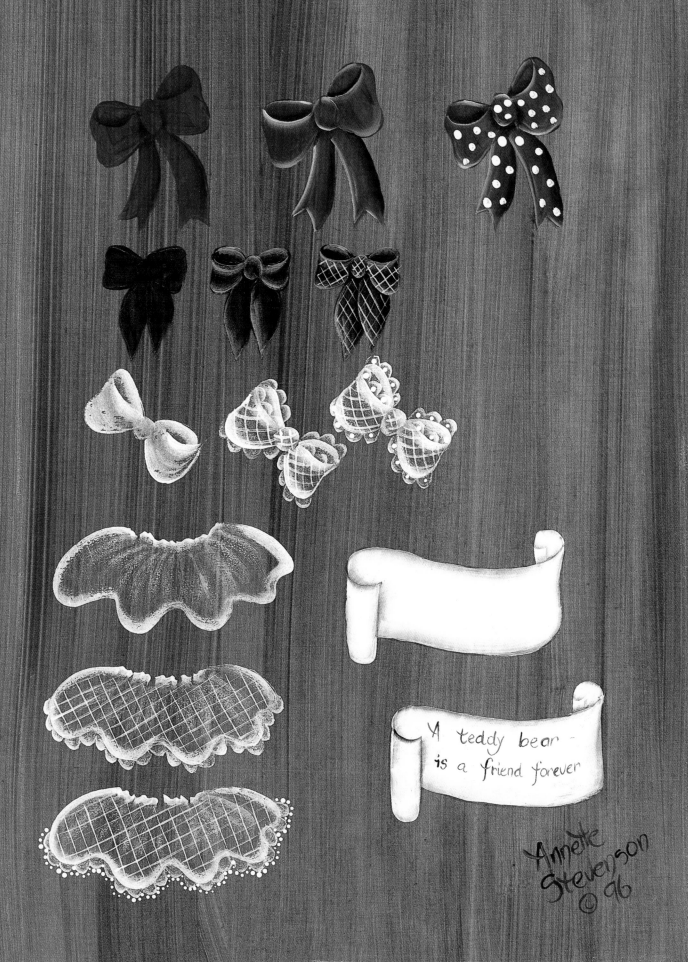

A teddy bear is a friend forever

WILLIAM AND THOMAS

This round box would make a wonderful treasure box for any little boy or girl.

MATERIALS

Oval ply box
1" sponge brush
Flat brushes, sizes 6, 8 and 12
Fine liner brush
Two rake brushes, size ³/₈
Three deerfoot brushes, size ³/₈
Stencil brush, size 8
Jo Sonja's Artists Acrylic Gouache: Raw
    Sienna, Burnt Sienna, Burnt Umber,
    Brown Earth, Yellow Oxide, Gold
    Oxide, Warm White, Paynes Gray
DecoArt Americana Acrylic Paint:
    Uniform Blue, Country Red
Matisse Professional Artists Acrylic
    Colour, Burgundy
Accent Faux Finish Decorating Glaze,
    Oak
Heart stencil (purchased)
Check stencil (purchased)
Sandpaper, 320 grade
White transfer paper
Stylus
Tracing paper, A4 size
Cabots Crystal Clear Varnish, satin
    finish

PREPARATION

See the painting design on page 64.

STEP ONE

I have stained this little box with an oak-coloured stain because I wanted a Baltic pine look. Brush this stain on with the sponge brush, following the wood grain.

STEP TWO

Paint the rim of the box lid with two coats of Uniform Blue. Apply the stencils to the side of the box. Stencil the checks in Uniform Blue and the hearts in Country Red.

PAINTING

THOMAS
(ON THE RIGHT)

STEP ONE

This is a fuzzy bear. Paint it in Burnt Sienna, shaded with Burnt Umber and Brown Earth brush-mixed together. Highlight with Burnt Sienna, Yellow Oxide and Warm White brush-mixed. Add extra Warm White highlights to his ears and muzzle.

STEP TWO

Paint the T-shirt in Warm White first, then add the Country Red stripes using the size 6 flat brush. Shade the white areas of the stripes with Raw Sienna and the red ones with Burgundy. The shading is under his chin, along the left side of the tummy and the left side of his sleeves.

STEP THREE

Paint his eyes with Burnt Umber and highlight them on the right side with Warm White so that he looks at William.

STEP FOUR

With watery Uniform Blue, paint the word 'BEAR' on his T-shirt on the third stripe down from his chin.

WILLIAM

STEP ONE

William is a long-haired bear and his colours are the same as in the general instructions for Long-haired Bear on page 7. Try not to paint him too dark.

STEP TWO

Paint his overalls Uniform Blue with Paynes Gray shading. Paint this down the outside edges of the straps, around both arms and around the outside edge of the pocket.

Keep the checks light so the stained background shows through

STEP THREE

Mix a small puddle of Warm White with a touch of Yellow Oxide to make a pale cream colour. Side-load a touch of this mix with Uniform Blue and float in the highlights on the straps, crotch, pocket and lower edge of the overalls.

STEP FOUR

Paint his eyes the same as Thomas's with the highlight on the opposite corner of the eye.

STEP FIVE

Using the cream mix and the liner brush, add buttons to the straps and a stitching line along the edge of the straps, down the front imaginary seam, around the inside edge of the pocket and on the bottom of the pants. Paint the letter 'B' on the pocket.

FINISHING

Because this box is made from craftwood, it is best to give the piece five coats of varnish, sanding between coats to ensure the surface is smooth.

William and Thomas are best mates

Painting Design
Note the painting design has been given at half size.
Enlarge on a photocopier at 200%.

64

SALLY

This painting case is one of my favourite pieces. The quaint old bear is so soft and cuddly with her roses and lace.

MATERIALS

Wooden case
Two rake brushes, size ¹/₂
Dagger brush, size ³/₈
Liner brush
Flat brushes, sizes 4, 10 and 12
Round brush, size 3
Stylus
1" sponge brush
Jo Sonja's Artists Acrylic Gouache:
   Raw Sienna, Brown Earth, Gold
   Oxide, Yellow Oxide, Burnt Sienna,
   Warm White, Pine Green, Smoked
   Pearl, Teal Green, Burgundy, Pine
   Green
DecoArt Americana Acrylic Paint:
   Buttermilk, Mauve
Liquitex Wood Stain: Dark Walnut,
   Cherry
Cabots Crystal Clear Varnish, satin
   finish
White transfer paper
Stylus
Tracing paper, A4 size
Soft cloth

PREPARATION

See the painting design on page 68.

STEP ONE

Mix the stain colour, using two parts of Dark Walnut stain to one part Cherry stain. Apply this with the sponge brush, then wipe it off with the soft cloth. Try to make this stain streaky to enhance the look of the timber.

STEP TWO

Trace the design and transfer it to the case, using the white transfer paper and stylus.

PAINTING

STEP ONE

This bear is painted following the instructions for Long-haired Bear on page 7 and in the same colours. Paint the entire body of the bear as the shawl is lace and the body should be visible through it.

STEP TWO

Base paint the hat in Raw Sienna, using the size 12 flat brush. Make the edge nearest her head a little irregular. Add some shading on the top of her head and on top of the hat rim, using Brown Earth side-loaded on the same brush. Float some highlights around the edge of the rim and the top of the hat, using a brush-mix of Raw Sienna and Warm White. Paint very fine lines of Brown Earth in a criss-cross pattern using the liner brush. It is helpful to water down the paint for these lines.

STEP THREE

Side-load the dagger brush in Buttermilk and float around the edges of the shawl. Float transparent lines across both sides of the shawl. Side-load the size 10 flat brush in Buttermilk and paint small C strokes to create the scalloped edge around the shawl. Using the liner brush and thinned Buttermilk, add some scallops to the top edge of each section of the shawl. Crosshatch between each of these sections. Do this very carefully so you do not put any lines inside the scallops. Finish the shawl with dots, made with the fine end of the stylus, around the scalloped edge.

STEP FOUR

The bow on Sally's head is painted in the same way as the shawl, with a floated edge, crosshatched lines and dots around the edge.

STEP FIVE

Paint the roses in the same way as the roses on page 15, but in slightly different colours. Base paint the roses with Smoked Pearl and Mauve. First shade with Burgundy, then with Pine Green. Paint the petals with Smoked Pearl, then with Warm White. Paint the leaves in Pine Green with a touch of Teal on the edge. Add the negative foliage, using a mix of Mauve and Pine Green.

FINISHING

Apply four coats of varnish to finish your lovely case.

Do not paint crosshatching inside the scallops

SALLY
Painting Design
Note the painting design is given at half size.
Enlarge it on a photocopier at 200%.

WASHING DAY

The whole family is all clean and fresh, hanging on the line. This lovely picture looks great on my laundry wall.

MATERIALS

Large frame 74 cm x 46 cm
  (30 in x 18 in)
Three deerfoot brushes, size ³⁄₈
Two rake brushes, size ³⁄₈
Three deerfoot brushes, size ¹⁄₄
Flat brushes, sizes 4, 8, 10 and 12
Fine liner brush, size 0 or 1
Round brush, size 2
1" base-coating brush
Fine sandpaper

Jo Sonja's Artists Acrylic Gouache:
  Raw Sienna, Burnt Sienna, Brown
  Earth, Yellow Oxide, Burnt Umber,
  Warm White, Fawn, Smoked Pearl,
  Teal Green
DecoArt Americana Acrylic Paint,
  Buttermilk
Matisse Professional Artists Acrylic
  Colours, Burgundy
Matisse Background Paint, Pale Beige
Blue transfer paper
Tracing paper, A4 size
Stylus
Cabots Crystal Clear Varnish,
  satin finish

PREPARATION

See the painting design on the Pull Out Pattern Sheet.

STEP ONE

Paint the inside of the frame with two coats of Pale Beige, sanding lightly between coats. Mix Raw Sienna with water and streak it across the background horizontally. A patchy finish is ideal for this piece.

Hanging out to dry!

70

Paint the frame with a 2:1 mix of Teal Green and Buttermilk. Sand back heavily to distress the frame, paying particular attention to the corners.

STEP THREE

Trace the design and transfer it onto the board, making sure that the design is centred.

PAINTING

BEARS

Paint the bears following the instructions for Fuzzy Bear on page 10 and Long-haired Bear on page 7. The instructions for the bears are numbered from left to right.

Bear 1: This is a fuzzy bear. Base paint it in Yellow Oxide, shaded with Burnt Sienna. Highlight with Warm White with a touch of Yellow Oxide. Base paint the T-shirt in alternating stripes of Teal Green and Buttermilk. Float in the shading with Teal Green, placed under the neck, down the left side of the T-shirt and sleeves. Wash a small amount of colour out onto the shirt so that you do not have a definite stripe of shading. Using the liner, paint the lettering with Burgundy.

Bear 2: This is a fuzzy bear. Base paint in Burnt Sienna, shaded with a mix of Burnt Umber and Brown Earth. Highlight with a mix of Yellow Oxide, Burnt Sienna and Warm White. Paint his tie with two coats of Buttermilk and float in some shading with a brush mix of Burnt Umber and Raw Sienna. This should be fairly faint. Add some Warm White highlights on the edges to lift the tie from the background. Using the smallest flat brush, or the round one if you prefer, add random checks in Burgundy.

Bear 3: This is a long-haired bear. Follow the colours listed in the basic instructions for this bear on page 7. This little lady only needs a small Burgundy bow. Float in a few highlights at the two top edges of the bow and to define the knot, using Buttermilk and Burgundy

brush-mixed together. Add the checks using the liner brush and watery Buttermilk.

Bear 4: This is a fuzzy bear. Complete this bear in the same colours as Bear 2. Paint the bow with Teal Green and float in some highlights with Buttermilk and Teal Green brush-mixed together.

Bear 5: This is a fuzzy bear. Paint this little lady in the same colours as Bear 1. Base paint her jumper and bow with a 2:1 mix of Teal Green and Buttermilk. Float in some shading using Teal Green and the largest flat brush that you feel comfortable working with. This shading is under the collar, down both outside edges of the sleeves and on the tummy, next to both sleeves. Highlight in the opposite areas using a mix of Teal Green and Buttermilk. This mix should look almost cream. Add fine lines with watery Burgundy, using the liner brush. Paint the dot flowers using the large end of the stylus and the highlight mix, with the centres in Buttermilk. Base paint her collar and skirt with Buttermilk and shade using Raw Sienna and Burnt Umber mixed together. Highlight with Warm White on the edges. Add a little scalloped edge using the liner brush and Buttermilk. Paint the stitching line around the collar and hem of the skirt in the mix used for the jumper.

Bear 6: This is a fuzzy bear. Base paint in Fawn and shade with a mix of Fawn and Brown Earth. Highlight with a mix of Fawn and Smoked Pearl. Add extra Smoked Pearl highlights on the tops of the ears, edge of the muzzle and the tops of the paws. Paint his shirt with Teal Green and float some shading with a mix of Burnt Umber and Teal Green. Highlight with Teal Green and Buttermilk to define all the folds where the peg is holding the shirt onto the line. Using the tip of the liner brush, add small stars in Buttermilk all over the shirt. These stars are painted as lots of fine lines all connecting in the centre.

Bear 7: This is a long-haired bear. Follow the directions and colours for this style of bear on page 7. Base paint the jumper with two coats of Burgundy, then shade with Burnt Umber floated with a flat brush. Separate the sleeves

from the body with a floated highlight of Burgundy and Buttermilk, brush-mixed together. For the Fair Isle pattern, add stitching lines with a mix of Teal Green and Buttermilk – this should be a light value. Add rough diamonds with Teal Green, painting the outside line of each diamond only. Add a smaller diamond inside these using the same mix as before. Paint the collar using the same colours as Bear 5.

CLOTHESLINE

Mix up a middle value grey, using Burnt Umber and Buttermilk. Load the round brush fully in this colour; side-load in Buttermilk on one side and Burnt Umber on the other. The rope is painted in one stroke – simply lay the brush down and lift straight off, repeating this action all the way along. The darkest side of the brush is facing down. If necessary, add a couple of extra highlights here and there with straight Buttermilk.

PEGS

Base paint these using Raw Sienna and the smallest flat brush. Float shading with the same brush and Brown Earth on the left side of each peg and the knob on the top. Add highlights to the right side and top of each peg, using a 1:1 mix of Raw Sienna and Warm White.

FINISHING

Varnish the picture with three coats of varnish and hang it in your laundry to brighten up your next washing day.

THE FAMILY

Mum, Dad, Jessica, Caitlyn, Samuel and Georgina are posed ready for the camera in this lovely portrait. The frame has been antiqued and distressed to give it the look of a charming old portrait.

MATERIALS

Large pine frame, 100 cm x 49 cm (39½ in x 19 in)
Jo Sonja's Artists Acrylic Gouache: Paynes Gray, Raw Sienna, Yellow Oxide, Brown Earth, Burnt Sienna, Warm White, Gold Oxide, Teal Green, Rich Gold, Burnt Umber
Matisse Background Paint, Pale Beige
Matisse Professional Artists Acrylic Colour, Burgundy
DecoArt Americana Acrylic Paint: Buttermilk, Uniform Blue
FolkArt Acrylic Colors: Peach Perfection, Cinnamon
Jo Sonja's Clear Glazing Medium
Liquitex Wood Stain, Dark Walnut
Two rake brushes, size ³/₈
Flat brushes, sizes 10 and 12
Liner brush
Round brush, size 3
Deerfoot brush, size ¹/₄
Filbert brush, size 2 or 4
Dagger brush, size ³/₈
Sandpaper, 120 grade and 320 grade
1" sponge brush
Stylus
White graphite paper
Tracing paper
Antiquing patina
Oil paint, Burnt Umber
Treasure Gold, Classic
J.W.'s Right Step Varnish
Soft cloth

PREPARATION

See the painting design on the Pull Out Pattern Sheet.

STEP ONE

Stain the main board with Liquitex Dark Walnut – this stain is a bit like jelly but has a beautiful depth to it when brushed on thickly. Use the 1" sponge brush to apply the stain and leave it quite streaky. Depending on the depth of colour that you want, add a second coat when the first is dry.

STEP TWO

Base paint the border with two coats of Pale Beige, then sand lightly. Base paint the outside of the frame with two coats of Paynes Gray. Sand this colour back to distress the frame in places – it is nice to see some raw wood on the edges – using first the coarse, then the fine sandpaper.

STEP THREE

Trace the design and transfer it, positioning the family in the centre of the main board.

PAINTING

Paint the bears as instructed for painting Long-haired Bear on page 7, working the ones that are behind, first. Once they are dry, Dad and Caitlyn are washed with a glaze of Burnt Sienna; Mum and Samuel are washed with a glaze of Yellow Oxide. The eyes and noses are painted in and you are ready to dress them.

DAD

STEP ONE

Base paint the hat and scarf with a 1:1 mix of Paynes Gray and Uniform Blue. Side-load the size 10 flat brush in a mix of Paynes Gray and Burnt Umber and float in the shadows along the seams of the hat and around the knot of the scarf.

STEP TWO

Paint the tartan check using the same flat brush loaded in the glazing medium and a small amount of Warm White. Make these fat lines follow the line of the fabric. Add fine lines in a mix of Paynes Gray and Buttermilk, using the liner brush. These lines are painted in between the previous ones. Stipple the pompom in Burgundy and add a touch of Buttermilk to it, using the small deerfoot brush.

STEP THREE

Base paint Dad's glasses with Raw Sienna using the round brush. Add some fine lines of Brown Earth here and there, for shadows. Finish with touches of Rich Gold for highlights.

MUM

STEP ONE

Using the dagger brush side-loaded in Buttermilk, float this colour around the outside edges of her shawl and bow. Float a small amount of the same colour under her chin.

STEP TWO

Side-load a size 10 flat brush in Buttermilk and float in the scallops along the edge of the shawl with little C strokes. Add fine Buttermilk cross-hatching lines inside the shawl and bow – these lines are straight, not curved. Finish with dots of Buttermilk made with the large end of a stylus. I find it best to do this when the picture is completed as there is less chance that you will touch the dots while they are still wet.

SAMUEL
(BETWEEN MUM AND DAD)

Base paint his bow with two coats of Paynes Gray. Side-load a small flat brush in a mix of Paynes Gray and Buttermilk and add the highlights – not too many as the checks will cover most of this. Add the checks with the liner brush loaded in the same mix.

GEORGINA (NEXT TO DAD)

Base paint the bow with two coats of Burgundy. Highlight with a mix of Burgundy and Buttermilk, side-loaded on the small flat brush. Add the dots with a small filbert brush and Buttermilk. There is no need to add shading to these bows as the base colours are so dark.

JESSICA AND CAITLYN

Float in Jessica's and Caitlyn's bows using Buttermilk and a size 10 flat brush. Both bows have crosshatching lines and dots in the same colour. The rose is painted following the step-by-step general instructions for roses on page 15. Paint a small rose on Jessica's bow. At the same time, paint another rose on Mum's shawl.

FINISHING

STEP ONE

Antique the cream frame with Burnt Umber oil paint and antiquing patina. Rub some Treasure Gold on the routered edge with the soft cloth, allowing some of the base colour to show through.

STEP TWO

Apply three coats of J.W.'s varnish to the picture, using a large flat brush.

Paint the fur on their tummies in a cross-hatched fashion

Annette
Stevenson
© 96

ACKNOWLEDGMENTS

Thanks: To my mum, Kate, for always being there when I needed you and to my husband,
Peter, for your constant love, support and humour.
Thanks also to my darling children, Jessica, Caitlyn, Samuel and Georgina, whom I cherish.
A special thankyou to Sue Schirmer, Sally Luck and Sue Iliov, my friends from the Victorian
Academy of Decorative Art, for all the encouragement and confidence you have given me.
To all my students: I thank you for the many hours of fun and laughter we have shared.
To Julie, my long-time friend and fellow bear-lover, thanks for your help in creating this book.
To David and Norma, for your wonderful pieces that inspire my work and for your friendship.

STOCKISTS

William and Thomas oval box is available from Timber Turn, 63 Booth Street, Panorama, South Australia 5041. Tel: (088) 277 5056

Blanket Chest, The Boys chest, The Family picture, Friendship Plaque, Claire book box, Madeleine picture, Chest of Drawers and the Washing Day picture are all available from Annette's Folk Art, 20 Sherwood Street, Glen Iris, Victoria 3146. Tel: (03) 9885 1101 or (Mobile) 0417 118507

Jack, the Hurt Teddy chest and the Françoise brush box are available from the Victorian Academy of Decorative Art, 1132 Toorak Road, Camberwell, Victoria 3124. Tel: (03) 9809 2788